Have You Considered
MANNERS

Marian Alydia Pilgrim

AuthorHouse™
1663 Liberty Drive
Bloomington, IN 47403
www.authorhouse.com
Phone: 833-262-8899

Because of the dynamic nature of the Internet, any web addresses or links contained in this book may have changed since publication and may no longer be valid. The views expressed in this work are solely those of the author and do not necessarily reflect the views of the publisher, and the publisher hereby disclaims any responsibility for them.

Any people depicted in stock imagery provided by Getty Images are models, and such images are being used for illustrative purposes only.
Certain stock imagery © Getty Images.

This book is printed on acid-free paper.

ISBN: 979-8-8230-0486-2 (sc)
ISBN: 979-8-8230-0487-9 (e)

Print information available on the last page.

Published by AuthorHouse 03/29/2023

authorHOUSE

Consider Jane Austin and her concern with the "manners" of her time in relation to the "manners" of today's technological information millennium erea. In Jane Austin Sense and Sensibility, one would find the next recommendation of Manners written by her and the Manners were particularly civil, allowing for some kind of sense, when I saw with what constant and judicious attention we were making ourselves agreeable to strangers. So with the technology research, some folks were only simple and just as the come-in to my view without any eclat. They were merely observed to be perfectly good-humoured and friendly. In some surprize at the familiarity of the question about technology or at least of the manner in ???which it was spoken, the answer was hilarious. The manner in which they had spoken increased my curiosity to find out more about manners in information technologies.

The principal attribute that preference of them which soon became evident in the manners of the people, who missed no opportunity of engagement in conversation and frank communication of technological manners made you think my questionings was odd. I dare say some of my friends and associates were personally acquainted with technological manners. When asked about manners in technologies, some people thought the question was very odd, and their countenance expressed it. So I wondered at the responses of some people, for I thought that the technologies they were holding in their hands were teaching them about some form of manners. Others thought it was a strange idea to enquire about phone manners when it is not the phone, but how the phone was used by the individuals. I taught for me to labour singly, to finish my research that evening, would work great, if it would allow me to share my works and was very obliged to everyone who participated for their help. Sometimes I found a bit of coldness and displeasure in the manner of the people that made me quite uncomfortable. While observing the people as they used their phones, I do not mean to say that I am particularly observant or quick-sighted in general, but in such a case, I am sure I could not be deceived with their phone manners. The eagerness to be gone declared the dependence on finding them there: and the resolve not only upon gaining every new light as to the character which her own observation or the intelligence of others could give to the situation, but likewise upon watching the behaviours of others with such

Technology or technologies is the branch of knowledge that deals with the creation and use of technical means and their interrelation with life, society, and the environment, drawing upon such subjects as industrial arts, engineering, applied science, and pure science. The synonyms for technologies include automation; machinery; computers; mechanics; mechanizations; robotics; telecommunications; applied science; electronic components; hitech; high tech; industrial science, scientific knowledge; scientific know-how technical knowledge.

Such information is for the application of this knowledge for practical ends and the terminology of art, science, ect: technical nomenclature, often lead to a scientific or industrial process, invention, method, or the like in which the sum of the ways in which social groups provide themselves with the material objects of their civilization. Thus one can even find Digital phone evangelism. There are scriptures such as Mark 13:1 that speaks of people going out of their worship places and questioning what manners of stone and what buildings were there. In verse 2, it showed "So ye in like manners when ye shall see these things come to pass knowth it is nigh, even at the doors." In those days zealous attention, as to be certain what was meant before many meetings had taken place. Show the results of the observation on manners in technologies be unfavourable, I decided to make all events open to other ideas. In a calm kind of way, with very little interest on either side, I encouraged them to talk about manners that they observed in the use of technologies both of them out of spirits, and the thoughts of both engaged elsewhere. This, on the manner in which it was said, immediately brought back to remembrance all the circumstances of quitting the project in the first place.

The next morning I recovered my spirit and was happy to look to continue my programme. It was a person so little known, to be carried on in so doubtful, so mysterious a manner! My colleague would represent in the strongest manner to me the necessity to continue my inquiry, while trying to entertain people with our project, we were all busy in observing the direction of the wind, watching the variations of the sky, and imagining an alteration in the air, as the people passing had not remained in this manner long before perceiving the people were standing within a few yards of them, in earnest conversation with their fashionable-looking phones. These were all young people that continued their discourse with one another. When one saw the look, his manner, had you heard his voice at that moment! One would think of 2 Chronicles 30:16 that speaks of "And they stand in their place after their manner, according to the law of Moses the Man of God: the priest sprinkled the blood, which they received of the hand of the Levites. So the manner of looking round the area, immediately made me fancy that they neither expected nor wished to see anyone there, and in short, that they were already aware of what occasioned their absence.

We had gone through the subject again and again; and with the same steady conviction and impetuous feelings and varying opinions as before, had to see whether the graces was of a polished manner as in this manner they had continued about a quarter of an hour. Soon they were startled by the manner looking anxious and saying what can be done, when the particulars of the conversation was repeated, the effect was not entirely such as the former had hoped to see. When the young person was called, speaking was voluntarily said, with a kind of compassionate respect, since everything within view would be bringing back the past in the strongest and most afflicting manner, by constantly placing people before the situation. Some of the questioning was very agreeable with manners which prevented them being generally pleasing: and capable of being sometimes out of humour perhaps might have passed over ???more had their manners been flattering to their friend. Such manners were not perfect, and so we had to encourage the manners we were hoping to see when using technologies. Thus we made some effort to preserve the good manners when we see each other using their apparatus (technologies) in a surprize, and felt that it must be great, as an address which, in words and manner, was assuming to them the right of first interest in the other person. To restrain them as much as might be, by their own manners, they were immediately preparing to speak. To speak for them in such a manner or to address in such a manner, there had been no real joy either in language or manners. Some of us was particularly struck with the very appearance and manners, which for the whole of the research had been depreciating, yet we believed everybody found their manners to be pleasing. Some were not often deficient either in manner or comprehension, so you were particularly struck by their manners before.

It was the first time observation that we were judging their general manners, and by inference, or the meaning of their manners towards us; of guessing how soon it might be necessary for them to throw coldness into our air; and of fancying seemed purposely made to humble them more, only brought amusement.

We had to force ourselves, after a moment's recollection, to welcome some people, with a look and manner that were almost easy, one almost open: and another struggle, another effort still improved them. Her manner gave some reassurance to us, and the courage enough to avoid embarrassment. That in the handsomest manner, for they loitered away several minutes on the place we were to meet. It was 2 Chronicles 32:28 that speaks of ???storehouses as with technologies also for the increase of corn, and wine, and oil: and stalls of all manner of beasts, and cotes for flocks. This therefore pointed us to what the technologies can do. I certainly should not have intruded on them in such a manner; though at the same time, we should have been extremely sorry to leave without seeing them. They were undoubtedly sensible people and they knew technology manners perfectly. Personally, I could not bear to leave the area in a manner that lead you, or the rest of the people, to suspect any part of what had really passed between them and us. Thus in Emma a classic romance by Jane Austin, the writer speaks of the person of unexceptionable character, easy fortune, suitable age, and pleasant manners, and there was some satisfaction in considering with what self-denying generous friendship they had. Whenever she was seen, there was always curtseys and questioning of how everyone was in a pretty manner; and working to observe their ways of doing things. Some had cheerful manners which always did them good with the use of their technologies. All manner of solemn nonsense was talked on the subject, but I believed none of it.

Some of my colleagues were much pleased with their manners as their person, and quite determined to continue the acquaintance. They would form their own opinions and their manners. We were not insensible of their manners, they had voluntarily noticed the other person's gentleness with admiration as well as wonder. Yet the other folks looked as if they did not know what manner was. When you compare their manners when using their technologies; of walking; of speaking; of being silent. One must see the difference that makes good manners the most valuable. They were not pleased the next day with the manner in which we seconded a sudden wish to have a picture with their technology gadgets. For the clownish manner which might be offending her every hour of the day, to know that they could write a good letter. To receive the assistance in the most comfortable manner. Some of those folks were pretty elegant people, of gentle, quiet manners, and a disposition remarkably amiable and affectionate. Their reserved what the observations of all might be, who were now seeing us together for the first time, might not have distinguished how we were by our look or manner. The technological questioning sometimes became one where we had to allow the people to understand whether it was the manners of the technology they were holding or they themselves and their manners. So we could not only love the blooming sweetness and the artless manner, but could most heartily rejoice in that light, cheerful, unsentimental disposition which allowed us so many alleviations of pleasure, in the midst of the pangs of disappointed joy. We were very struck with the loveliness of the people's faces and warm simplicity of their manner; and all the probabilities of circumstance and connection were very favourable. Such expression, assisted us as we were by everything that look and manner could do, made us feel that we had never valued highly what we were doing. They were rather good; their face not pretty; but neither feature, nor air, nor voice, nor manner; were elegant. But the manners did appear immediately, but no, they would not permit a hasty or a witty word from themselves about their manners. For there really was nothing in the manners of either but what was highly conciliating. We could not begin to understand that even Luke 1:29 had a depiction of when she saw him, she was troubled at his saying, and lost in her mind what manner of salutation this should be. Even Luke 1:63 reminded us that we can see technologies been used as "And he asked for a writing table, and wrote, saying, His name is John. And they marvelled all." Also

Luke 1:66 speaks about "And all they that heard them laid up in their hearts, saying what manner of child shall this be and the hand of the Lord was with him." So we can see that under a peculiar sort of day, blunt manner, we knew one can find the warmest heart. One conscience can tell that it was not the same cheerful volubility as before - less easy of look and manner. The intention, however, was indubitable; and whether it was that the manners had in general so little gallantry, or however else it happened, but that taught nothing.

Once the research had began we also felt that reading Jane Austin books and seeing the era that the works was written can be seen in the now as been very useful when we examine the manners of the time. Some folks spoke in a manner which seemed to promise us many particulars that could not be given now. Some entered on the subject in a manner to prove, that they now only wanted time and persuasion to think their engagement with us was not a very bad thing. Such was some of them having indeed quite a different manner toward us, a manner of kindness and sweetness making us aware of it. To be pained by the manner in which they had been received. Such manner, perhaps, may have as little to recommend them and here we can admit, that the manners to them was being unpleasant and highly blameable. To be very kind, I knew what my manners were to everyone.

When it came to the manners in technologies it seemed already beginning, and in a most gradual, natural manner that Jane Austin Pride and Prejudice; Mansfield Park; Persuasion; Emma and Northanger Abbey had its linked to many areas of manners in that era and today's technological times. So each areas of careful writing had to be intermingled with some of the ancient works that shared such manner of reading. This for example will be shown in 2 Chronicles 34:13 that states, "Also they were over the bearers of burden, and were overseers of all that wrought the work in any manner of service: and of the Levites there were ???scribes, and officers, and potters. In Ezra 5:4 we read "Then said we unto them after this manner, what are the names of the men that make this building? or that build this building? But woe unto you, Pharisee! For ye tithe mint and rue and all manner of herbs, and pass over judgement of the love of God: these ought ye to have done, and not to leave the other undone" (Luke 11:42) "Yet they sent unto me four they kept the feast seven days; and on the eight day was a solemn assembly, according unto the manner. So Persuation is comparatively light-textured book, lacking the rich ironies of Emma that fold equivocation and insight into every page of the work, making the reader work for and against Emma's understanding. But Persuasion is a book about a longed-for and impossible return. Also Nehemiah 10:37 speaks of "The fruit of all manner of trees". "And he said unto them, what manner of communication are these that ye have one to another, as ye walk, and are sad? (Luke 24:17). "And there were set there six waterpots of stone, after the manner of the purifying of the Jews, containing two or three firkins apiece." (St. John 2:6). (Nehemiah 13:15 & 16) "Also wine, grapes and figs, and all manner of burdens. An all manner of wares." "For so was the King's manner towards all that knew law and judgement" (Ester 1:13). "What manner of saying is this that he said, ye shall seek me, and shall not find me: and where I am, thither ye cannot come?" (John 7:36). "Then look they the body of Jesus, and wound it in linen clothes with spices, as the manner of the Jews is to bury (St. John 19:40). "Which also said, ye men of Galilee, why stand ye gazing up into heaven? This same Jesus, which is taken up from you into heaven, shall so come in like manner as ye have seen him go into heaven" (Acts 1:11) In Romans 6:19 we read "I speak after the manner of men because of the infirmity of your flesh: for as ye have yielded your members servants to unclearness and to iniquity unto iniquity: even so now yield your - members servants to righteousness unto holiness." In Acts 13:18 there is a saying that "about the time of forty years suffered he their manners in the wilderness." "And is the first day there shall be an holy convocation, and in the seventh day there shall be an holy convocation to you: No manner of work shall be done in them, save that which every man must eat, that only be done of you." (Exodus 12:16). "And certain men which came down from Judea taught the brethren, and said, Except ye be circumcised after the manner of Moses, ye cannot be saved." (Acts 15:1). "And they wrote letters by them after this manner." (Act 15:23). Thus the manners in technologies stretches to the entire areas of our lives. So that Pride and Prejudice (1993) Wordsworth Editions Limited.

Speaks "in a manner of a detective" where she goes back over the evidence, searching for the clues that was missed before. The voice, countenance and manner of her time was established on the possession of every virtue. These disclosure on the following manner of the pleasant countenance, and easy, unaffected manners were shown to remain, until the manners gave a disgust which believe, than those of any other set of beings in the world. But the difference in their manner of doing things could not be unfelt. The composed mind and polite manners of the people were put to some trial on this point, in the intercourse in the city, and it was a question which, in a more rational manner, neither one thought unimportant.

Sometimes we are to remember that some folks have the technologies in their hands, while others have to wait for their technologies to be given to them. So good company requires only birth, education and manners, and with regard to education is not very nice. Birth and good manners are essential, and with manners as consciously right as they were invariably gentle; turned again their, and by manner, rather than words, was offering the services to them. Your person, your disposition, accomplishments, manners are all described and was presented to me. People tried to avoid any such alteration of manners as might provoke a remonstrance on their side. And the manner in which it had been received, a manner of doubtful meaning that the manner to themselves might have spared them much or all of this, meant that they cared not much for the people, and had nothing to blush for in the public manners of what their parents believed. That because their manners had not suited the others own ideas

They had been too quick in suspecting them to indicate a character of dangerous impetuosity; and that became the manners that had precisely pleased them in their propriety and correctness, their general politeness and suavity, that their had been to quick in receiving them as the certain result of the most correct opinions and well regulated mind.

The texts of four of the novels are necessarily based on the first edition: in the case of Pride and Prejudice. Emma did not reach a second edition in Britain in Austin's lifetime; and Northanger Abbey and Persuasion were published post-humously. Sense and Sensibility and Mansfield Park, however, both appeared in second editions in which Austin took some part. All these editions have been read and from them have formed my works on the consideration of Jane Austin works. She was born in December 16, 1775 and from a family of 5 (2 boys & 1 sister). She died on 18 July 1817 in Winchester, where she had gone for medical attention, and was buried in Winchester Cathedral. Three of her novels set up intellectual and moral debate in their titles: two of them are Sense and Sensibility and Pride and Prejudice. The third Persuasion. Arguments within classical philosophy and stories of the Bible suggested the double-tongued dangers of Persuasion. Thus Nehemiah 8:18 speaks of "And times after this sort: and I answered them after the same manner. Then sent Sanbalat his servant unto me in like manner the fifth time with an open letter in his hand." (Nehemiah 6:4???) And Luke 30:31 speaks of "And the third took her; and in like manner the seven also; and they left no children, and died." Such words in the scriptures has had it effect on the reading and writing of Jane Austin works. In Persuasion we find Jane Austin had the Penguin edition and it chronology with its ways that the person had always loved and relied on, could not, with such steadiness of opinion, and such tenderness of manner, be continually advising her in vain. There was hardly any personal defect, replied the person, shortly, an agreeable manner. May set off handsome features, but can never alter plain ones. When the dear person recollect what a comfortable account was sent to me of themselves writing in the cheerfullest manner, and said we were perfectly well on our way with the project, we were in no hurry to rush the work. Todays children had more modern minds and manners. In the pass even their dress had every advantage, their faces were rather pretty, their spirits extremely good, their manners unembarrassed and pleasant, they were of consequence at home, and favourites abroad. We were at the right time and right moment to take up our own cause, and the sincerity of our manner being soon sufficient to convince them, where conviction was at least very agreeable. To keep our eyes open on the subject, we had to remember that manners come in every daily kind of living and so we had to have eyes but for them, as to the manner of living on board, daily regulations, food, hours ect. Because a short absence from home had left us unguarded by the attention at the most critical period in our work, and when we came back to doing our research, we had the pain of finding very few people with altered manners, and of seeing us. We had little to triumph after the people with technological manners had no pitiful triumph in their manners. When some folks came in this manner on purpose to ask us, how can one say no? And in short, we look and declared that we ourselves need to used our technological gadgets in the manner that we wanted them to answer us. Some of those same respondent said they would be so much pleased with their mind, that we would very soon see no deficiency in our manner. Our manners were so exactly what they ought to be, so polished, so easy, so particularly agreeable, that they could compare them in excellence to only one person's manners. As to what is necessary in manners to make people quite the thing, are more absurd, I turned the tide of popularity, and made one discovered the pride and arrogance of being seen with one technological gadgets. Remember Acts 17:2 speaks "And Paul, as his manner was, went in unto them." Romans 7:8 Reminds us "But si??? taking occasion by the commandment, wrought in me all manner of concupiscence. For without the law sin ??? dead." When technologies are not in use, and the gadgets are not plugged into its source, most of the time I hate to see people standing by themselves in a stupid manner without having a happy manners that shows that their manners are not equal to them. They were at the same time haughty, reserved, and fastidious, and their manners though well bred, were not inviting.

Some of the way the manner in which they spoke of the other people was sufficiently characteristic of their way of saying that their pleasing manners grew on the goodwill of not only the user of the technologies but both the people and the technologies. A composure of temper and a uniform cheerfulness of manner which would guard one from the suspicious of the impertinent. And in spite of their asserting that their manners were not those of the fashionable world, they were caught by their easy playfulness. It had given them likewise a pedantic air and concerted manner, which would have injured a higher degree of excellence than they had reached. So when there were no questioning, you would be considering how insupportable it would be to pass many evenings in this manner in such society; and indeed I am quiet of your opinion. As one listened to them with perfect indifference while they chose to entertain themselves in a manner that was composed. Thus one was convinced that all was safe as long as our wit flowed long. Sometimes we had to ask questions that can collect the manner of their talking, you must become two of the silliest people in the country, and in their brother's manner there was something better than politeness; there was good humour and kindness. Even though some people manners were pronounced to be very bad indeed, a mixture of pride and impertinence; their was no conversation, no style, no taste; no beauty. Such a countenance, such manners and so extremely accomplished for their ages, that when asked or pressed about manners in technologies, some possess a certain something in them as to the air and manner of speaking as well as tone of voice that to address the question and receive expressions, or the word will be but half deserved. We had to remember where we were and tried not to run in a wild manner that cause us to suffer embarrassment, or to be offended by our manner of mentioning a country, place, neighborhood or area that the people own easy manners recommended them had increased into assurance. Yet their was a mixture of sweetness and archness of their manner which made it difficult for us to affront anyone. If they were carried on in a different manner, but if they will listen to the information, then they may perhaps be a little softened by the manner of expressing themselves, their air was grave and stately, and their manners were very formal. The subject on manners elevated them to more than usual solemnity of manner. And the subjection in which the people had brought them up had given them originally great humility of manners.

On their return to the highly gratified ways of admiring manners and politeness to the technological ages that is now in this millennium, some people were happy to know that the next person finally seated themselves and their was an agreeable manner in which they immediately fell into conversation that was agreeable after receiving the answer, asked in a hesitating manner how long the individual have been using their phone (or technologies). So then we were able to know that they were connected with the use of the technologies and the particular manner from infancy. We were well surprised, at such an assertion, after seeing as you probably might, the cold manner of our meeting yesterday. The world is blinded by the fortune and consequence, or frightened by the high and imposing manners, and sees the only area they chooses to be seen. To treat in such a manner anybody who had probably been the only one from childhood to be connected to their technologies in the closest manner can make one think if or when their manners were dictatorial and insolent. But I rather believe that people derives part of their technological abilities from their rank and fortune, part from their authoritative manner, and the rest from pride. We can see in one's conversation the manners recommended by them to everybody. But when one consider in what a disgraceful light it places the person, to be treating the favorite person in such a manner as they spoke at length in a constrained manner. Such person is blessed with such happy manners as may ensure them making friends and in a manner which they are likely to have less suffering in the use of their technologies in life even though they were treated in a most infamous manner. It all started with a weak voice that affected their technological manners. And I do not think it of light importance that he should have attentive and conciliatory manners towards everybody, especially towards those to whom they owes their preferment. This was because they had set about thinking about technological manners in a very orderly manner and soon found that it was their manners that was been described and not the use of their technologies. Whose negative might be uttered in such a manner as must be decisive. Though their manner varied however, their determination never did. And if their manner had been at all reprehensible, I here beg leave to apologised to everybody. But by stiffness of manner and resentful silence, they were allowed to sport with it in whatever manner they thought best. The alteration of some of their manners would allow them to deceive themselves no longer for by their manner of talking on their technologies, one can wish them all manner of evil. Acts 20:18 says "And when they were come to him, he said unto them, ye know, from the first day that I came unto Asia, after what manner I have been with you all season. And Acts 22:3 states "According to the perfect manner of the Law of the Fathers." And in their manner of bidding one another adieu. Thank Heaven I left them where I found them and met another set of agreeable quality of people who had neither manner nor sense to recommend them as they instantly saw that their cousin's manners were altered by them not been able to use their technologies when they would like, and have been restricted due to the work place situation that they had found themselves from that knowledge of what manners of the great really are, which my situation in life has allowed me to acquire. Such formidable accounts of those people, and their manner of living left one to think of the introduction that was performed in a proper manner, without any of those apologies and thanks which would have been thought necessary. The air was not conciliating, nor was the manner of receiving from them, such as to make one forget such a person in their inferior rank. In a manner which they all would bear as they deliver their opinion on every subject on the question of technological uses in a decisive manner as to prove they were used to have their judgement controverted. Their manners were very much admired at the scene. Speaking of the use of the technologies in a masterly manner as an instrument move with the fingers holding or touching it, they saw there was less captivating softness in the way their manners might have the best informed mind. Acts 23:25 says "And he wrote a letter after this manner. As she spoke, she observed that we were looking at her earnestly, and the manner in which she immediately used her technology we supposed the person likely to give them any uneasiness, convinced them that they had somehow or other got pretty hear the truth about how they were good with the use of technologies than they themselves taught that manner; not often united with great sensibility.

They could not have appeared with propriety in a different manner. With manners so far from right itself, was entirely insensible of the evil. Our plain manner of living, our small area of concern, and the little we see of the world. It was delivered in a sentiments of a manner so suited to recommend them. There was such an expression of goodness in their countenance! Such an openness and gentleness in their manner. I shall merely be able to tell what the person may tell in a much more agreeable manner themselves without the unguarded and imprudent manner. That on their making some enquiring as to the manner in which their time had passed at the place. Their manners were very different from the others. I did not mean that either their mind or manners were in a state of improvement. In as guarded a manner as one could. But the embarrassment of their manner spoke volumes about the use of their technologies. But there was a sense of good humour in her face, and her manners were perfectly unassuming and gentle. As convinced her that the improvement of manners which she had yesterday witnessed. And whose own manners indicated respectability, was not to be hastily rejected. To forgive all the petulance and ???acrimony of her manner in rejecting him. Or any they could. Some of them were determined to ??? what manner that their friend was to be happy using their technologies so as to make them happy. Their understanding excellent, their mind ???improved and their manners captivating. In an hurried manner they immediately began to enquire if one health can be used in this technological era? Some people have agitated manners and then one can use their technologies to speak for them. While some behaved in a more expected manner without agitation. Yet some people manners were open, cheerful, and engaging as even, some had unfeeling manner. While others had manners of impressing me with the fullest belief of their arrogance, conceit, and a selfish disdain of feelings for others. To me the young people's manners in society were always engaging. And it has taken many, many years since I first begin to think of technologies in a different manner. To promote this advancement in the best manner that my profession might allow, is speaking in what manner I do not know and under what form of falsehood to impose on people. The countenance, voice and manner, had to be established at once in the possession of every virtue. As proud and repulsive as we their manners, they had never, in the whole course of their acquaintance, an acquaintance which had latterly brought them much together and there was a constant complacency in the way there unsettled in the extreme. Though at first she often listened with an astonishment bordering on alarm, at her lively, sportive, manner of talking to her brother. Therefore Pride and Prejudice, which opens with one of the most famous sentences in English literature, is an ironic novel of manners. In it the garrulous and empty-headed Mrs. Bennet has only one aim - that of finding a good match for her five daughters. In this side is marked by her cynical and indolent husband. With its wit, its social precision and, above all, its irresistible heroine, Pride and Prejudice has proved one of the most enduringly popular novels in the English language. Acts 26:4 also states "My manner of life from my youth" enabled me to see the way manners and technologies have interlinked during this New Millennium. And one can continue to take a deep look at the "manners" then and the "manners" of today.

any peculiarity of manner, where their two sets only were concerned.

After sitting in this manner a quarter of an hour. Acts 25:16 reminded me "It is not the manner of the Romans to deliver any man to die. And Acts 25:20 stated "And because I doubted of such manner of questions! Their pale face and impetuous manner made them start to understand what their technologies had to them. Who, in a manner which though it spoke compassion, spoke like wise restraint. She had been allowed to disposed of her time in the most idle and frivolous manner, and to adopt any opinions that came in her way. And I flatter myself they will settle so quietly, and live in so rational a manner, as may in time make their past imprud??? forgotten. Their manners had improved. And how far??? and cold was their manner, whenever they did. I have said no such thing. I am only resolved to act in that manner. Never had his wit been directed in a manner so little agreeable to her. Had you behaved in a more gentleman-like manner. My manners must have been in fault, but not intentionally I assure you. After walking several ???miles in a leisurely manner. She could not help smiling at his easy manner of directing her friend. It was certain that her manner would be equally ill - adopted to do credit to her sense. Their manner of living, even when the restoration of peace dismissed them to a home, was

6-12 YEARS

Sports
Technologies

001 0-3 YEARS

PRAM

3-6 YEARS

Talking Books

SECONDARY SCHOOLS

Science & Technologies

WONDERFUL APPS

- User experience

- Impact on lives.

- Iphone = Be Real (Social media) sensation that gives us an authentic look into the lives of our friends and family.

- Game of the year = Apex Legends Mobile.

- Ipad app of the year = Good Notes

Game = Moncape

Mac App = MacFamily Tree

Game = Inscryption.

Apple watch app = Genlter Streak

Apple TV game = El Hijo

Arcade game of the year = Wylde Flowers

NB Things that didn't Exit on Christmas 20 years ago: Iphone, Facebook; YouTube; Instagram; Twitter; TikTok, Android; Bitcoin; Tesla; Ipad; G-mail; Netflex streaming; Amazon prime; Slack; Reddit; Etsy; Whats App; Messenger, Google Maps; Snapchat; LinkedIn; Pinterest; Chrome; Zoom; Skype, Spotify; Airbnb, Uber (Jon Erlichman)

Oldest to pass exam.. at 92

TOP GRADE Grandad Derek Skipper

GRANDAD Derek Skipper has become the oldest person ever to pass a GCSE – getting a top grade in maths at the age of 92.

The ex-RAF radar fitter was "very, very pleased" with his grade five, the highest possible mark for the foundation paper he took. He signed up to the eight-month course last autumn to "keep my mind occupied" during the winter.

The pensioner from Orwell, Cambs, did classes via Zoom on the course run by the Cam Academy Trust in Cambridge.

He said: "Like most people who don't understand maths much, it gave me the opportunity to learn something."

As a schoolboy during the Second World War he missed just one day of classes, when a bomb blew his front door on to his bike and gave it a puncture.

He earned five School Certificates – the precursor to O-Levels, which gave way to GCSEs – including maths.

He says: "Now having done it as a mature student, it all does make a bit more sense."

He is urging others to sign up to classes, but adds: "I think that is going to be my lot – I am going to retire now."

Mirrow
Friday 26/08/2022

Mirrow
Friday 26/08/2022

—— Stay clear of groups of negative - "Himnies" and "Debbie Downers" or they will sure going to bring you down with the sinking ships with them."

—— "Rather than wait for those out-of-body experiences where you suddenly realize how much certain person or group of people have shaped your life for better or for worst, stay alive and think carefully about the people or group!"

—— "We need to think of how our loved one and friends get their daily recommended average (RDA) of social connectedness with other human beings."

—— "Some guests and intruders have friends faces and good hearts, some have pretty faces but ugly hearts, others have pleasing aesthetic designs, and others have "credibility"."

—— "Ongoing physical exercises."

—— Given that information about our emotional state is encoded in our heart's electromagnetic field, perhaps that transfer of electromagnetic energy carries useful information to us about other people to help us sum them out or make decisions."

—— "There is clearly another form of communication in our world that is unseen and unheard, and the heart is implicated."

—— In pursuit of civility manners and civilization in Early Modern England by Keith Thomas (2018; 2020) Yale University Press New Haven and London.]

—— 19th Century "European states sought to define the conditions on which they would admit other countries to membership of international society, they invoked a "standard of civilization" to which Asian and African governments were required to conform if they wished to be recognized

Between 1530-1789 enquiry that was taken (*1900-2000) enquiry into manners and civility can become a part of an attempt to construct an historical ethnography of early modern England which has occupied me on and off for many years. As an outsider, a stranger by birth an and alien by choice, I have tried to study the English people in the way an anthropologist approaches the inhabitants of an unfamiliar society, seeking to establish their categories of thought and behaviour and the principles that governed their lives. The aim is to bring out the distinctive texture and complexity of past experience in one particular milieu. (1) Early modern notions of good manners (2) Changes (3) I consider how far those ideals remain relevant in modern times and ask whether social cohesion

only that you can please and consequently rise". It was said that Good Manners, helped to keep the peace in families, among neighbors; and throughout the nation. Today the 13th of July 2022 it was at the EE phone store that the true advantage of business as noted in a contemporary historical form in the 16th Century, that the individual () showed herself affable, smooth and courteous. She stood behind the counter in all courtesy civility, and with "good manners". In this New Millennium defenders of the commercial interest would argue that trade refined and polish "manners," because it encourage more extensive contact with the rest of the world. It is how a time for educational responses in regards to teaching the people how to use their phones and how to up simultaneously with the improvement of technology in the Arts, Manufactures, and Commerce. "Manners" therefore meant to be ready to engage, insinuate, shining manners, where one is able to distinguished politeness, an almost irresistible address; a superior gracefullness in all that is done or said. It is possible then that there be a tension between "Manners" as an agent of social differentiation and "Manners" as a source of peaceable living today. To find a theory that explains the spread of "good manners, we need to look at the new technological ages we are living in, and the people in the nation who need to deal with each other and not cause displeasure by having more manners when they use their gadgets. Such growth of human interdepen Manners today, way the information technology is used by everyone. "Good Manners, in the sense of considerate behaviour and tactful accommodation to the feelings of others, continue to be widely regarded as serving an essential purpose. That is it or information technology facilitate communication between human beings. The Psychology of "Manners" according to Jessie Ware and Gennie Ware Table Manners The Cook Book Ebry Press (2020) Penguins Random House Co –– Instead of holding a knife & fork lets hold a phone or an Information system in our hands. Introduction; effortless; A Bit more effort;people or culture;

–– Let see the gadgets and how the young people behave with be heard or seen in shown on the CNN Broadcast the 06/08/2022 The technology of the Metrological Advancement had the weather personnel in stiches, yet with "Good Manners" they were able to carry out the weather focus with a polite laugher and even though there was fellow laughter from other colleagues, the main personnel was able to give the focus of the weather and the are from where he was living had a polite "manner" about how the technology was handled.

12/08/2022

–– Cellphone evangelism that runs through AWR 360° (For more information on how to get involved, visit: https://awr.org/training/)★

–– Dictionary.com

–– Manner (Noun) A way of doing, being done, or happening; mode of action, occurrence, ect. –– The prevailing customs, ways of living, and habits of a people, have manners that my holiday visit to London Bridge, where it was noticable that many visitors were walking about with phones on a stick and asking to be excused as they held up their phones on the stick as they went by. This was my first though about the use of "Manners" when using the information technology to me. From then it was necessary for me to observe the way people moved and held their phones as the travel. Of course I always made an effort to look and ask the person what was the instrument that they were using and the way they took hold of the situation was always amazing to me. According to Jessie, she remembered using emails to get her friend to go out on a first date. And also to get music from her phone. Such was the "Manners" that show through become educated in the "Manners" needed in the use of the phone in the New Millennium. According to Keith Th regarding Archbishop Harsnet two scho At Cheqwell, Essex, in 1629, he declared that he was more concerned that the scholars should have been "nurtured and disciplined in "good manners" than instructed in good arts." John looked agreed that priority should be given to teaching "Manners" and good habits: that was indeed "the main point" of Education. Even the clergy saw "good Manners" as an important in the lives of everyone h sociable "Manners" and conversation. E the magistrates of the law was used to refor people's "Manners." So with the New Millennium here, we can have a quick glance at the past and see that never in the history of the world, have there been a more progress made refinement of Manners and Moral's going also assists the brain's plasticity and, amongst other things, increases the size of the hippocampus, a region involved in memory and stress regulation."

—— "Sleep helps us to consolidate memories and reduce the intensity (Amydala) of emotional events, helping us to better regulate our emotions the following day."

—— "Smells can also affect our thoughts and behaviours when we're not even consciously aware of their presence, let alone that they're influencing us. Smells can trigger mental associations we have which then influence our behaviours."

—— "Water and nutritious food are to us what petrol or diesel and water are to a car: vital for functioning!"

—— "Dopamine might be trying to nudge you in the right direction. (A feel good brain chemical) (ROI) Returns on investment"

happiness are possible without good manners to reinforced the prevailing social structures in this New Millennium. <u>NB</u> See Early Modern, then changes in this era! "It". Today the concept of the chronology of "Manners" can be defined by how one uses the "phone" that they possesses. So now we have to teach our children to learn "Manners, as they call the information technology". At the same time, the term "Manners" also continue to be used in the older and much wider sense of the customs, morals and mode of life prevailing in any particular society. An for me in the narrowest sense of conventions governing personal interaction that one can call "decency of behaviour", that my thesis would take a closer look at today. We have to look at the involvement of tactful behaviours on our phones, the repression of anger and insult, and a determined attempt to reduce combativeness in our social interactions with each other. Everyone can expect to display tolerance. Mutual respect as sovereign bodies. This was a updated version of the "ius qentium" law of nations, which had been invoked by jurists in the early modern period. Naturally, it was a standard that embodied the legal and political norms of Western Europe. It made no allowance for alternate cultural traditions. If other peoples failed to meet its formal criteria, international law denied them recognition as sovereign states and permitted foreign intervention in their domestic affairs."

—— "I have tried to be sensitive to chronological change, but I have not hesitated to "bunch" evidence drawn from different centuries when that seemed justifiable."

—— "In the eighteenth Century, Britain developed the most advanced economy in the world and extended its empire into other parts of the globe." Now that it was people truely have the "Manners" to deal with each others "phone" and the way of life in this New Millennium. For though "good manner" might indicate genuine benevolence towards others, they were usually a diplomatic way of concealing one's true feelings. Thus a way to please others when one comes in contact with one another. Moreover, when one seek to make oneself agreeable to others this often leads from a frank, not to say cynical recognition that this could help one to get on in life. Erasmus had regarded "good manners" as a sign of inner virtue, that everyone thought that it was an external business. So when people had to say anything unpleasant about anybody it would always be behind their back, out of pure "good manners." Which is compatible with personal wickness as the puritans would claim. To celebrate good sun came out.

–– At miday however, a few specks of sm rain gave me the joy of meeting people with their phones (computers caught without try to avoid my watchful eye, and "Oh! dear, I do believe I am wet," broke from one of my respondent in a most responding tone.

–– If it keeps raining, the streets would be very wet and with umbrellas up already people would only wipe their phones and seek their own shelter.

–– It was such a nice looking morning. I felt so convinced it would be dry!

–– The next morning there was a new area that was not to be easy till I had explained everything.

–– While talking to each other, I observe with some surprize that the person, who was never in the same part of the area for 5 minutes speaking was engaged in conversation with another person who also, graceful, I should not be shy.

–– Reserve! - how in what <u>manner</u>? What am I to tell you? What can you suppose?

–– The reservedness of his <u>manner</u> towards her contradicted one moment what a more animated look had intimated the preceding one.

–– Technology was the subject which ensured my attention, and was the beginning of describing my own admiration of it and questioning more minutely on it was interesting.

–– To understand people who pretend to more admiration of the beauties of nature than they really feel, and is disgusted with such pretensions, he affects greater indifference and less discrimination in viewing them himself than he possess. One has to be gadgets in hand.

TECHNOLOGICAL ADVANTAGES

Because of technological advances of the twentieth and twenty-first centuries, research studies are revealing that "good manners" are more important to not only to our way of life, but to our environment as many people previously thought. Lets explore why "good manners" is imperative today. During quality time one cannot be distracted with the notifications on their electronic gadgets. Children with the help of their parents, can set up their own media platforms to share what "Manners" that they have learnt from their parents, school, church ect. anything that they would share about their phone. But we must allow for difference of taste, so therefore some people had to be overlooked. Yet everyone that I tried to question to me must be a person with <u>Manners</u> that ornament their goodness with every possible charm.

—— I come back tired to death sometimes when I go to do a few interviews in the towns and cities.

—— By the shake of the people's head, one can tell that they wanted to not think of their own phone/computers.

—— Everywhere was to be seen in different areas at different periods of the fashionable hours: Crowds of people were every moment passing in and out, up the steps and down; people whom nobody cared about, and nobody wanted to see, but me that was looking at everyone with their phones/computer coming

—— I asked people about their phone, but as soon as I was just going to ask again, some folks turned round and was gone! - that is a cursed shabby trick!

—— Not those who bring such fresh feeling of every sort to it, as they does.

—— In chatting with people before the evening concluded, a new source of felicity arose to me.

—— Some mornings brought a soberness as the sun made only a few efforts to appear. And as augured from it, everything most favourable. A bright morning allowed generally for some rain to fall but a cloudy one fortold improvement as the day advanced. There was no doubt in the world of its being a very fine day, if the clouds would only go off and the And walked up the hills in speed; we walked along the roads and met many people at a spot which we had never happened to reach any in our walks before.

—— The person received the kindest welcome from me; and shyness, coldness, reserve could not stand against such a reception, and they were quite overcome by the captivating <u>Manners</u> of my colleagues that assisted in the observation and research.

—— Sometimes one is guided by what people say about themselves, and very frequently by what others people say of them, without giving oneself time to deliberate and judge.

—— People are guided wholly by the opinion of other people.

—— If I could persuade myself that my manners were perfectly easy and Anxiousness to question them more.

—— Never satisfied with the day unless it was spent in conversation with people about the use and <u>manners</u> of their tech.

—— The matter or <u>manner</u> would not disgust the people who love their technology conversation.

—— They met me following a conversation which took place between appointments

—— These <u>Manners</u> did not please.

—— The very easy <u>Manner</u> in which the individual kept you waiting for an answer, did not by any means reconcile you to do any particular ideas.

—— The <u>Manner</u> some folks had shewed good sense and good understanding of their knowledge about their phone/computers. They were neither shy, nor affectedly open to tell whatever was asked, without exaggerated deal delight or of morality, a religious duty to live "honestly and civilly." It was also said that religion was the form that made us to have the best "Manners" in the world. Yet we need to become educated in the use of our knowledge about the technological advances in our hand and for the future! As was indicated the concept of Manners is universal, yet it differs from culture to culture and from time to time are its specific manifestations. In this age of technology, the idea is to find someone whose manners, facial expressions and gestures had been fashioned into a work of art marked by elegance and self-control. What about foreign travel? Have the information age reached everyone? How have they used their manners? Therefore both males and females ought to have the "Manners" of Technological usages; looking at the development and self-control by behaving in such a way as to ease the task of living in harmony with their fellow human beings. So to have "Manners" in the ordinary parlance, is to behave in a decent, law-abiding fashion. Thus it involve consideration and accommodation to the needs of others, and is a social phenomenon rather than a written one. And so today in this New Milllennium a new departure in the history of Manners are been seen in a wider moral and intellectual context with an emphasis on a form of manners that is of a self-presentation on the level of social harmony. Thanks to technology "manners" have gained a much wider readership than previously. All stratified societies have their rules of etiquette and self-control that was and still is in existance long before there was a printing press invention. It can be noted in the statutes for Oxford College gossip, not boasting about oneself; avoiding pedantic, technical or disputatious issues, and if one had to contradict others; we are to have "good manners and never allow disagreement to jeopardize the personal relationship. Gossips was potentially too disruptive. Now that Manner in the social order can be interpreted as nothing else but the modesty and decorum to be observed by everyone according to their condition. It is important to take a concise look at the social behaviours of people on a whole to see whether their "manners" are seen to please everyone around them. Our "Manners" require behaviours appropriate to the time, place and occasion. Thus the ages and their sex (male or female) would be looked at to see how their phone manners are applied to their everyday living. Would women and men, boys and girls <u>Manner</u> imaginable.

–– The people immediately made the matter perfectly simple by assuring me that tech was entirely owing to the peculiarly judicious <u>manner</u> in which the travel was done was in a singular discernment.

–– to move in the same quiet <u>manner</u> without showing the smallest propensity towards any unpleasant vivacity.

–– My reassurance to those that I met was that their <u>manners</u> would recommend them of their sex, but in spite of this, the extreme weariness of their company, which crept over them before they had been able to answer.

–– Some folks had a thousand things ??? moment's conversation fastidious and will have to have an affectation of their own.

–– Everyone pretends to feel and tries to describe with the taste and elegance of him who first defined what picturesque beauty was.

–– I detest jargon of every kind, and sometimes I have kept my feelings to myself, because I could find no language to describe them in but what was worn and hackneyed out of all sense and meaning.

–– Sometimes one can become confused, yet could not help but smile at the quiet archness of the people <u>manners</u> after a moments of silence.

–– Never had any week passed so quickly, we could hardly believe it to be gone.

–– Our profession engaged our time and gave generations using their gadgets or phone/technologies have been using their phones in a respectable <u>manner</u> as to engage the general good opinion of their surrounding acquaintance.

–– Every day brought its regular duties: - shops were to be visited; some new part of the town to be looked at; and the areas where people paraded up and down for hours, looking at everybody and speaking to no one with their phones in their hands; some on poles or sticks held high up in the air. Once the people was talked to with fluency and spirit and there was an archness and pleasantly in their <u>Manners</u>, I was interested to understand after chatting sometime on such technological matters as naturally arose from the objects around us. Thus the attachments used for the ears and the (published 1818, Penguin English library.)

–– "Years have passed since it was finished, many more since it was begun, and that during that period, places, <u>manners</u>, books, and opinions have undergone considerable changes.

–– When meeting technology savvy people on their way with their phones or computers their "heart was affectionate, disposition cheerful and open, without conceit or affectation of any kind - their <u>manners</u> just remove from the awkwardness and shyness" of a person trying to please and explain the ignorant and uninformed researcher like myself in questioning mind.

–– It is now expedient to give some description of the people that the reader may be able to judge, in what <u>manner</u> the actions would in their hands.

–– Far more ready to give - than to receive information, and hearing what the people were saying.

–– When people expatiated on the beauty of their phone or related their different situations and views.

–– The conversation turned upon the subjects, of which the free discussion has generally much to do in perfecting a sudden chat about phone <u>manners</u>.

–– Every home with an information piece of technology can be seen when everyone is out of their inhabitations, and all the world appears on such an occasion to walk about tell their acquaintance what a charming day it is to breathe the fresh air.

–– In morning lounges or evening assemblies, among walkers or travel can be seen people with their phones, to which my imagination around the person and manners increase my inconceivable vexation on every little trifling occurrence.

–– Then I had to walk about, and quiz people.

–– Everyday when I awoke perfectly revived, in excellent spirits, with fresh hopes and fresh schemes to deal with the research. The first wish of my heart was to consider Jane Austin and her concerned with the "manners" of her time in relation to today, and almost the first resolution, to seek for that purpose in technological information and its people's "manners."

–– At 9 am in the morning is a final time to watch everyone hurrying to their place of duty with their gadgets (phone, computers ect) in hand, from babies in pushchairs to workers using their tech as they go to their places of work or journeys in the quietest

The knew that the conversation with a stranger would never happen again, so with smiles of most exquisite misery, and the laughing eye of utter despondency, I bade the people adieu and went on.

–– To smile incredulously, and talk the rest of the evening to those that passed by with their phone, to ascertain whether they had <u>manners</u> in the use of their phones.

–– My resolution to meet or endeavouring to meet as many people in the morning or evening again continued in full force, where the course of events and conversation took place, and walked in that <u>manner</u> for some time.

–– In the end of the day there was then an object of expectation, the future looks good for the information technologies as more and more gadgets are now that was founded by Bishop Richard Fox in 1517, that some of the rules stated that members should avoid all forms of insulting behaviours and strive to live lovingly together, for there was nothing more necessary for the community than proper manners. (Morumbonesta) so that courtesy, self-restraint and mutual respect can be obtained wherever the "phone" is used nowadays in this nineteenth and twentieth century with the discussions of good "manners." It was the 17th Centure theologian Henry More that said that manners was a virtue and that we are reminded that everyone has a common link to each other and therefore we each have to have a cheerful voice, countenance and gesture to talk to whosoever we meet, so that when they ask us how we are, they too can think of themselves the better for asking. According to Keith Thomas (2020) "Good manners thus came to be seen as a branch of of gadgets that are present on stream, we would see hand-held and on-hand-held accessories for the use of all "phones". The majority can be access from all the different countries of the world. This is good for trade and now we can obtain many of the needed requite from China and America and the rest of the European countries. According to Keith Thomas, it was David Hume who claimed that it was "in order to render conversation and intercourse of minds more easy and agreeable" that "good manners" had been invented. In his day the term "conversation" could still refer to social intercourse of any kind, its narrower meaning of spoken exchange between people had long been familiar. So today when we use our "phone" it is the "good manners" in our conversation that matters. We are to transmit information that is helping us to make everyone agreeable to others. On our "phones" we are to be interesting and amusing; not interrupting; not engaging in malicious be the same when using the phone? As Whichcote said in Keith Thomas's writing we have to consider the ages, places, relations, functions, education, and to proportion themselves according to their "manners" in society. Such assumption to treat others according to how we perceive them, can be an enduring strand to the concept of using the information technology to seek out what "manners" can be in this New Millennium. But having read what was said by Robert Ashley in the 15th Century, "It is part of civil courtesy and modest humanity to speak gently to all, to salute, embrace and entertain them without difference." With the phone in our hand a "dextrous management of our words and actions, whereby we make others people have better opinion of us and themselves." It is by manners an interest of our plans and actions. Some inconveniences to our friends, indeed, might result from it - you would not be able to give others as much of your time.

–– But with a smile we would benefit in particular at least to know where to go when we left them.

–– Her <u>Manners</u> were by no means so elegant as the rest, but were much more prepossessing.

–– Some folks smile when they came, smiled all the time when they spoke; some only stopped smiling when they laughed and smiled when they went their way.

–– In the morning excursion to meet others in London we met many people from various countries walking over the swing bridge. Their dress was very smart, their manners very civil.

Printed in the United States
by Baker & Taylor Publisher Services